Around the World
Festivals

Margaret Hall

Heinemann
LIBRARY

www.heinemann.co.uk/library

Visit our website to find out more information about **Heinemann Library** books.

To order:

☎ Phone +44 (0)1865 888066

▤ Send a fax to +44 (0)1865 314091

▭ Visit the Heinemann Bookshop at www.heinemann.co.uk/library to browse our catalogue and order online.

First published in Great Britain by Heinemann Library, Halley Court, Jordan Hill, Oxford OX2 8EJ, a division of Reed Educational and Professional Publishing Ltd. Heinemann is a registered trademark of Reed Educational and Professional Publishing Ltd.

OXFORD MELBOURNE AUCKLAND JOHANNESBURG BLANTYRE
GABORONE IBADAN PORTSMOUTH NH (USA) CHICAGO

Designed by Lisa Buckley
Originated by Dot Gradations
Printed in Hong Kong/China

ISBN 0 431 15130 X
06 05 04 03 02
10 9 8 7 6 5 4 3 2 1

British Library Cataloguing in Publication Data

Hall, Margaret
    Festivals. – (Around the world)
    1. Festivals – Juvenile Literature
    I. Title
    394.2'6

Acknowledgements

The publishers would like to thank the following for permission to reproduce photographs: Title page, p.28 Eye Ubiquitous/Corbis; pp.4, 5, 8, 13, 18, 25 Joe Viesti-The Viesti Collection; p.6 T. Black/Robert Harding Picture Library; p.7 Akira Nakata/Haga Library Inc.; pp.9, 14 Hideo Haga/Haga Library Inc.; p.10 Pierre Hussenot/CEPHAS; p.11 Tom McCarthy/Index Stock Imagery; p.12, 29 AFP/Corbis; p.15 Novosti, London; p.16 Hideto Sasamoto/Haga Library Inc.; p.17 Carol Beck and Angela Fisher/Haga Library Inc.; p.19 Daniel Czap/CEPHAS; p.20 Annie Bungeroth/Panos Pictures; pp.21, 22, 23 Haga Library Inc.; p.24 Richard T. Nowitz/Corbis; p.26 Earl and Nazima Kowall/Corbis; p.27 Marcus Rose/Panos Pictures.

Cover photograph reproduced with permission of AFP/Corbis.

Every effort has been made to contact copyright holders of any material reproduced in this book. Any omissions will be rectified in subsequent printings if notice is given to the publishers.

Contents

Some words are shown in bold, **like this.** You can find out what they mean by looking in the glossary.

Festivals around the world

All around the world, people have festivals to **celebrate** special days. These festivals are about the **customs**, **culture** and **religion** of the people who celebrate them.

Festivals are times for family and friends to be together. Whole **communities** or countries may celebrate at the same time.

Spring festivals

Many festivals are **celebrations** of different seasons. In the spring, people **celebrate** the way things begin to grow again after the winter.

There is a big **bonfire** at some spring
festivals. People feel that the fire
is chasing winter away. They may also
burn something that stands for winter.

Summer festivals

There are festivals to **celebrate** the warmer weather and longer days of summer. There are even festivals that celebrate Midsummer's Day, the longest day of the year.

Many flowers grow in the summer. People often wear **costumes** with flowers and leaves on them for summer festivals.

Harvest festivals

People have had **harvest** festivals for thousands of years. These **celebrations** are ways to give thanks for the food that people grow and eat.

Many crops are ready to be picked in the autumn. That is when most harvest festivals are **celebrated**. People often share huge **feasts** as part of these festivals.

Winter festivals

Winter nights are long and dark in many places. People often **celebrate** winter festivals by lighting candles.

Even when the weather is cold, people like to celebrate outside. They may have winter festivals and play games in the snow and ice.

New Year festivals

Different **cultures** begin a new year at different times. Whenever their new year starts, people **celebrate** it. They have **parades**, parties, **feasts** and fireworks.

Everyone hopes for good luck and happiness in the new year. Some people celebrate by going out to visit neighbours and friends. They wish each other a happy new year.

Festival clothes

Many people wear special clothes for festivals. They may get new clothes to wear. They may wear the **traditional** clothing of their **culture**.

People sometimes dress up in **costumes** to **celebrate** a festival. They may wear masks or paint their faces. They may paint other parts of their bodies too.

Festival food

Families and friends like to **celebrate** festivals by eating together. The meals they share usually include **traditional** foods.

Foods are traditional when they have been part of the **culture** and the festival for a long time. Older people teach younger ones how to cook them.

Music and dancing

People often sing songs and play **musical instruments** at festivals. Bands play music and march in **parades**.

Festivals are also times when people like to dance. Many festival dances are very old. They are another way to show the **customs** and **culture** of a group.

21

Independence festivals

People all around the world are proud of their country and **culture**. They often show their pride by having festivals with **parades**, speeches and fireworks.

Many countries have festivals to **celebrate** their freedom, or **independence**. They also have **ceremonies** to remember important things that have happened.

Religious festivals

Some festivals are **religious celebrations**.
People go to **religious services** as part of these
festivals. They may also eat certain foods or
wear festival clothing.

People **fast** for some religious festivals.
This means they do not eat for a time.
In some **cultures** there is a carnival
when people wear masks and **costumes**
before the time of fasting.

Nature festivals

Some festivals **celebrate** the power
of things in nature. People may light
candles for festivals of the sun or the
moon. Many of these festivals started
long ago.

People also have festivals to ask for things they need. They may want rain for their crops. They may hope for plenty of fish and other animals to hunt for food.

Fun festivals

Some **celebrations** are just for children. In Japan and Turkey, these festivals are called 'Children's Day.' Children receive gifts and have parties.

Other festivals are very different. People do things like get soaking wet or dance on **stilts**. Every festival is a special way to celebrate.

Photo list

Glossary

bonfire fire in an open, outdoor area

celebrate have a party or do something special

celebration party held for a special event or holiday

ceremony special words and actions that are used on important days

community group of people who live close to each other and do things together

costume special clothing that makes the wearer look like someone or something else

culture things that a group of people does and believes in

custom way something has been done for a long time

fast go without eating for a time

feast special meal at which many kinds of food are served

harvest pick crops when they are ready to eat

independence freedom from being ruled by another country

musical instrument something used to make music, such as a drum, flute or guitar

parade group of people who march on foot or ride on vehicles to celebrate an event

religion what a person believes about God

religious service meeting or event where people gather to practise their religious beliefs

stilts tall pieces of wood that people use to walk on

traditional handed down from one person to another over a long period of time

More books to read

Dat's New Year by Linda Smith, A & C Black, 1994

Diwali by Linda Smith, A & C Black, 1994

Eid ul-Fitr by Linda Smith, A & C Black, 1994

Festivals Through the Year series by Anita Ganeri,
    Heinemann Library, 1999

Sam's Passover by Linda Smith, A & C Black, 1994

Index

Titles in the *Around the World* series include:

Hardback   0 431 15120 2

Hardback   0 431 15130 X

Hardback   0 431 15121 0

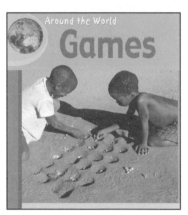

Hardback   0 431 15131 8

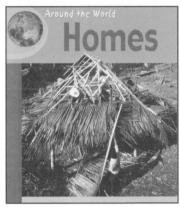

Hardback   0 431 15122 9

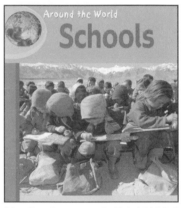

Hardback   0 431 15132 6

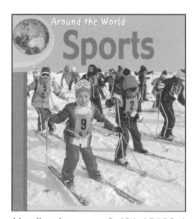

Hardback   0 431 15133 4

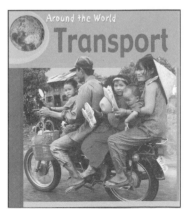

Hardback   0 431 15123 7

Find out about the other titles in this series on our website www.heinemann.co.uk/library